I0473025

ILLUSTRATED FLORAL
LETTERS
─ COLORING BOOK ─
ALL 26 LETTERS OF THE ALPHABET IN FLORAL ART

Illustrated by
PHILIP BOELTER

Inspired by the lettering community and the beauty of floral illustrations, I found a passion in combining both to create something fun for people to color.

I hope you enjoy spending time coloring the letters of the alphabet. I love seeing everyone's personalized works of art, so feel free to share your own pieces online and remember to tag @BoelterDesignCo.

Thank you to my friends, family, and my wife for all the support through countless nights spent fulfilling my dream of creating a coloring book for everyone to enjoy.

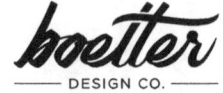

boelter
─ DESIGN CO. ─

Copyright ©2016 Philip Boelter
ISBN-13: 978-0692634271

First Edition

www.BoelterDesignCo.com

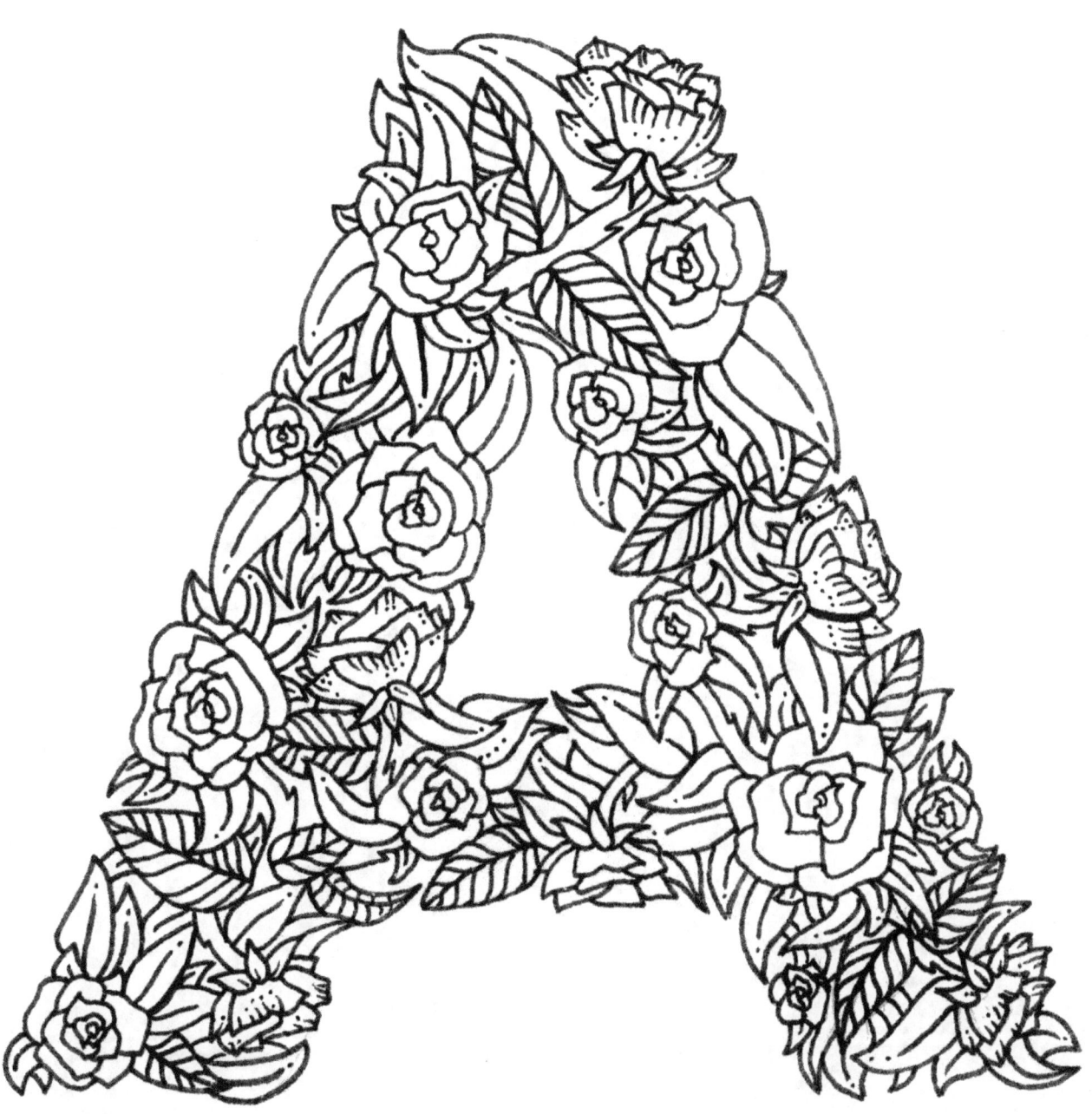

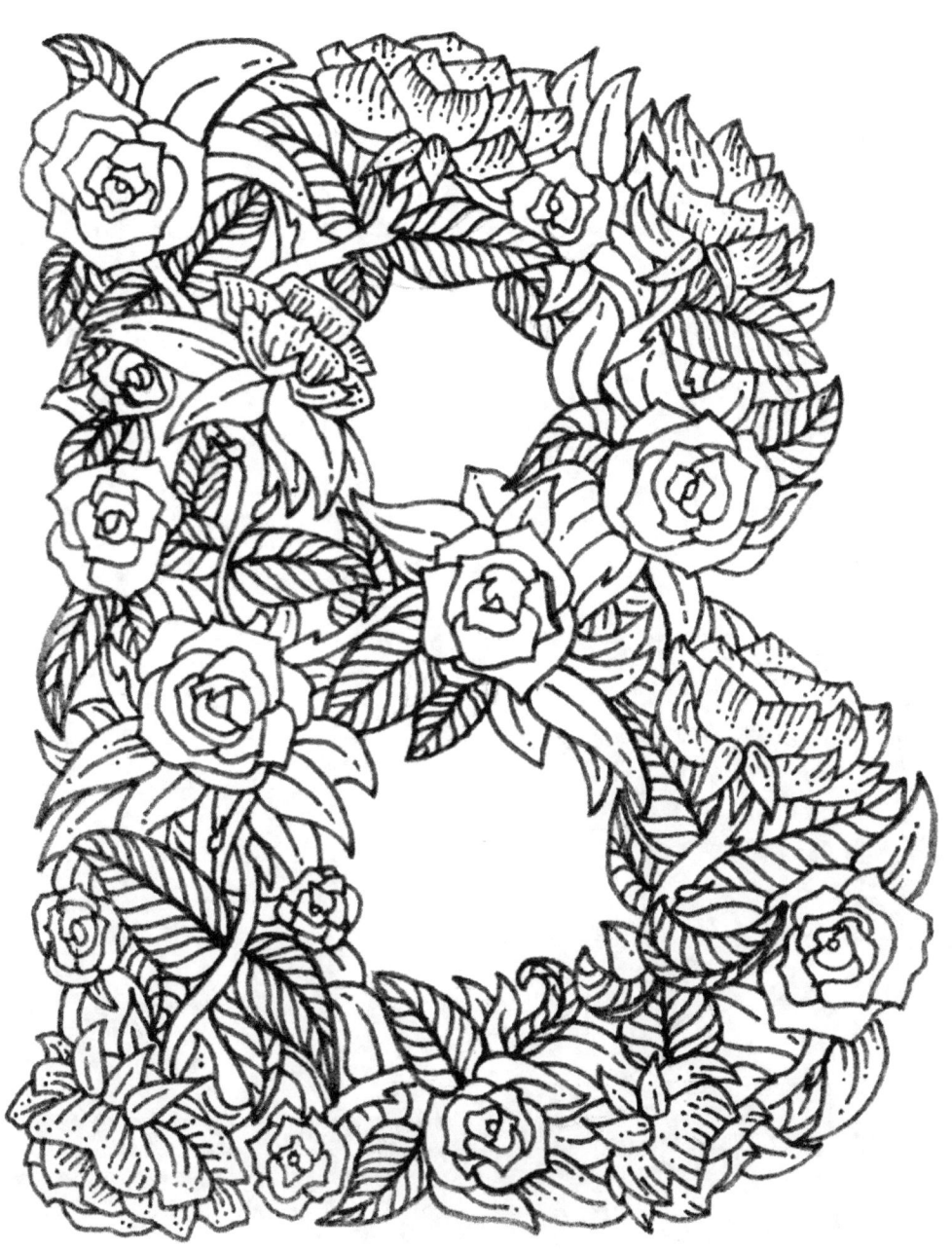

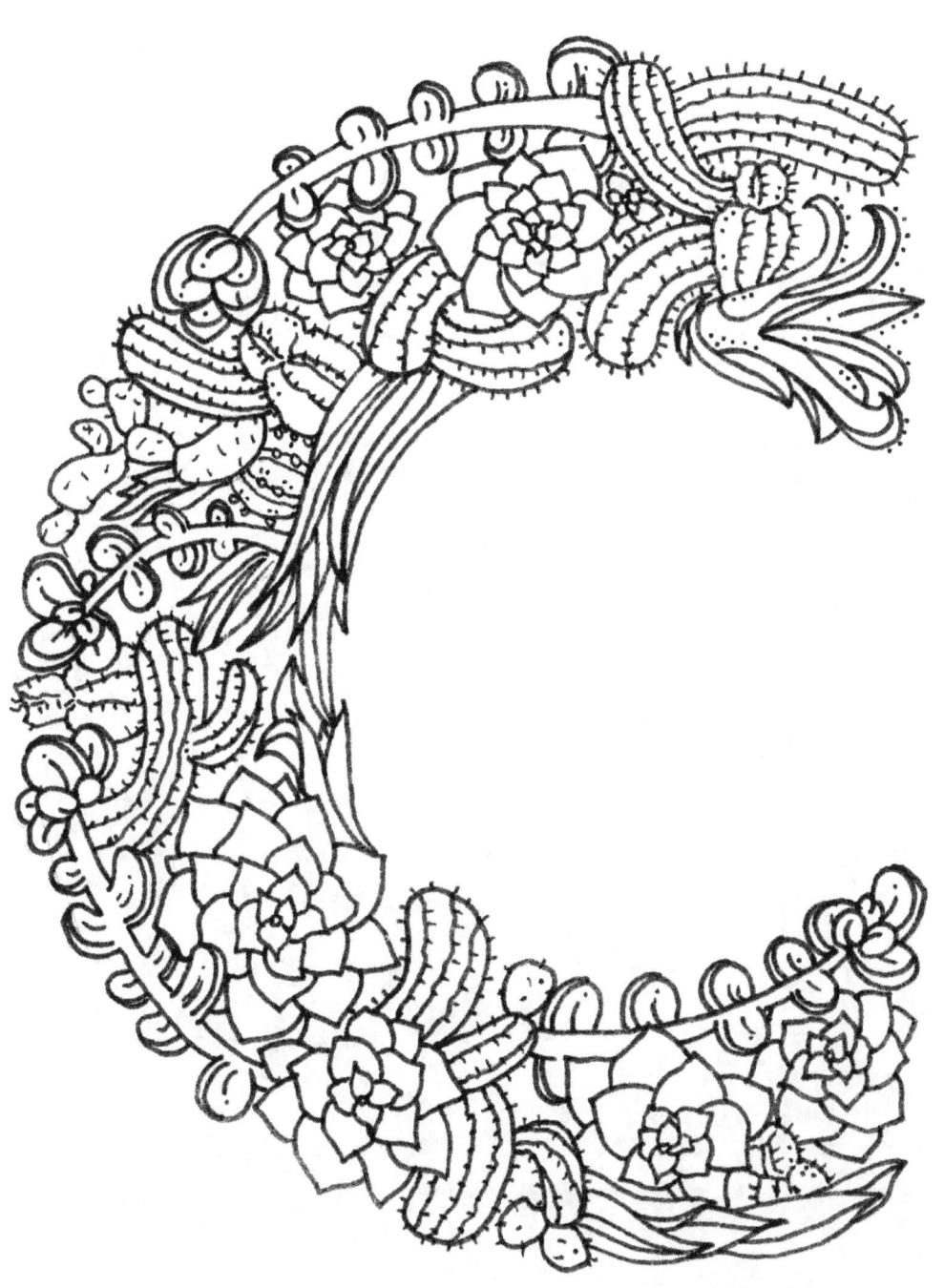

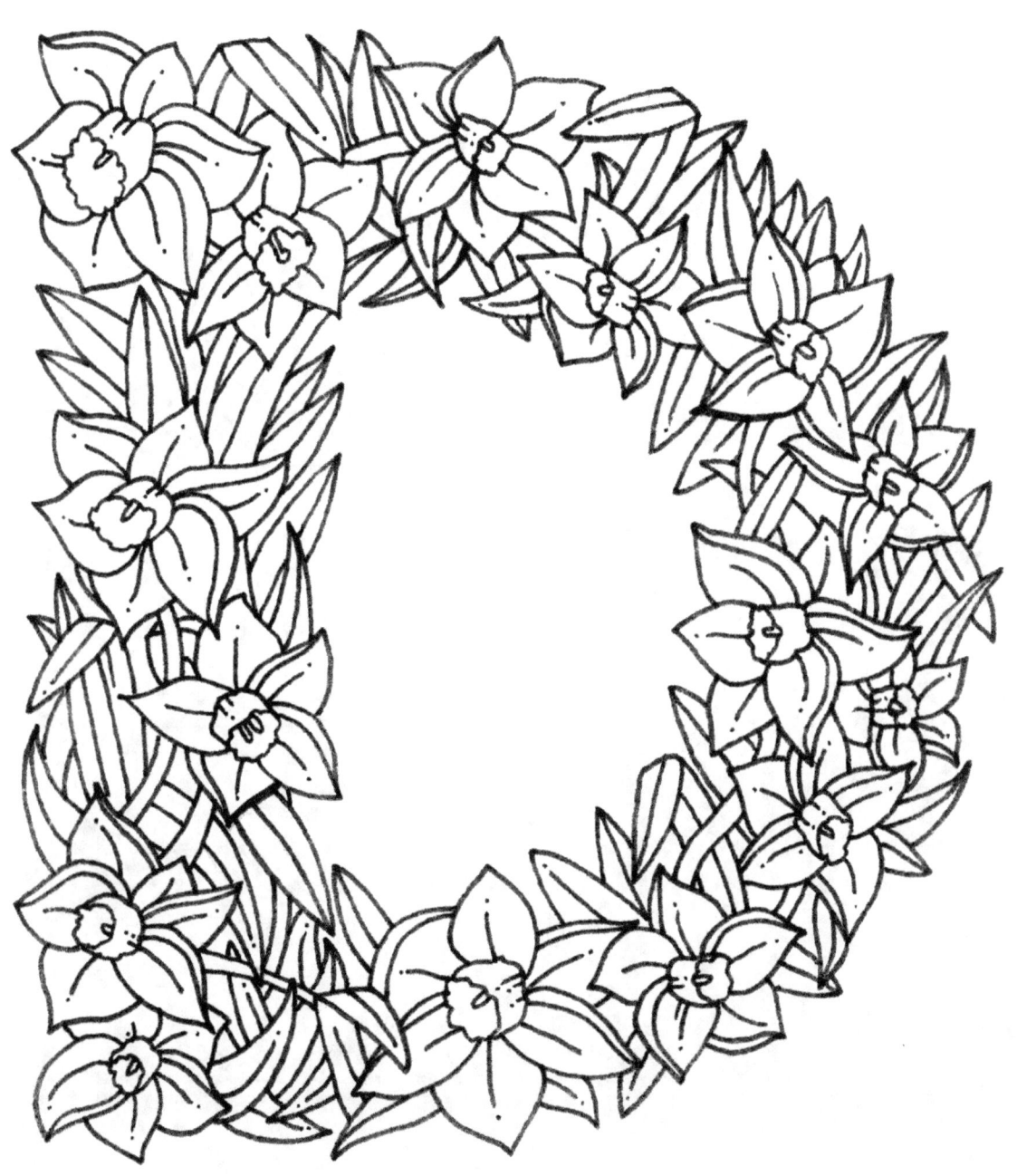

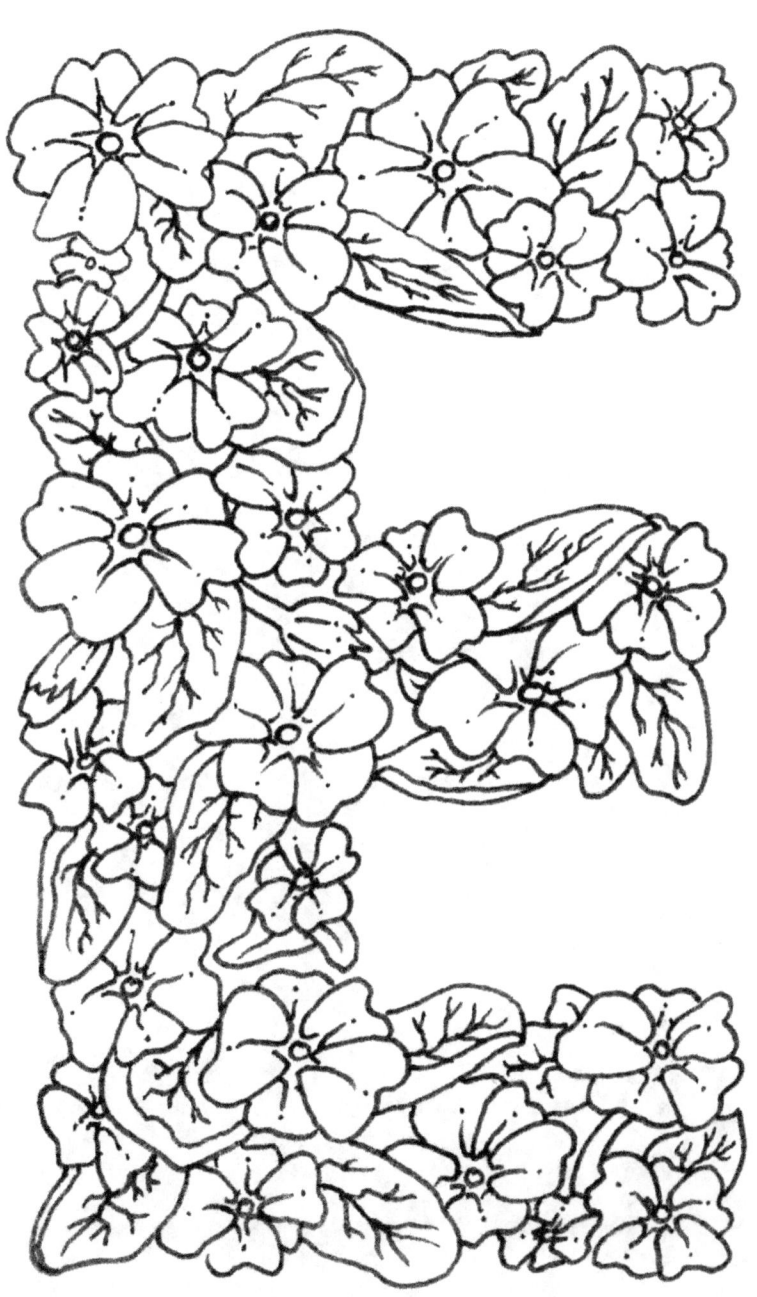

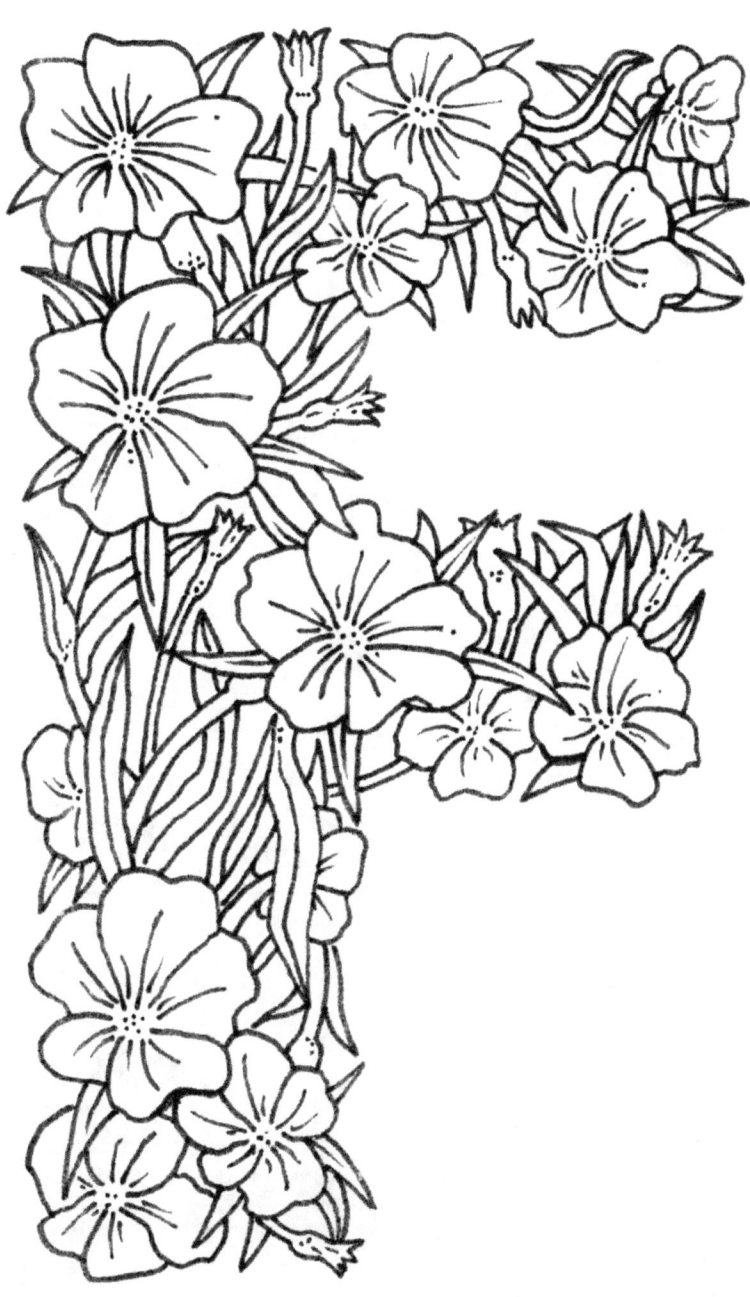

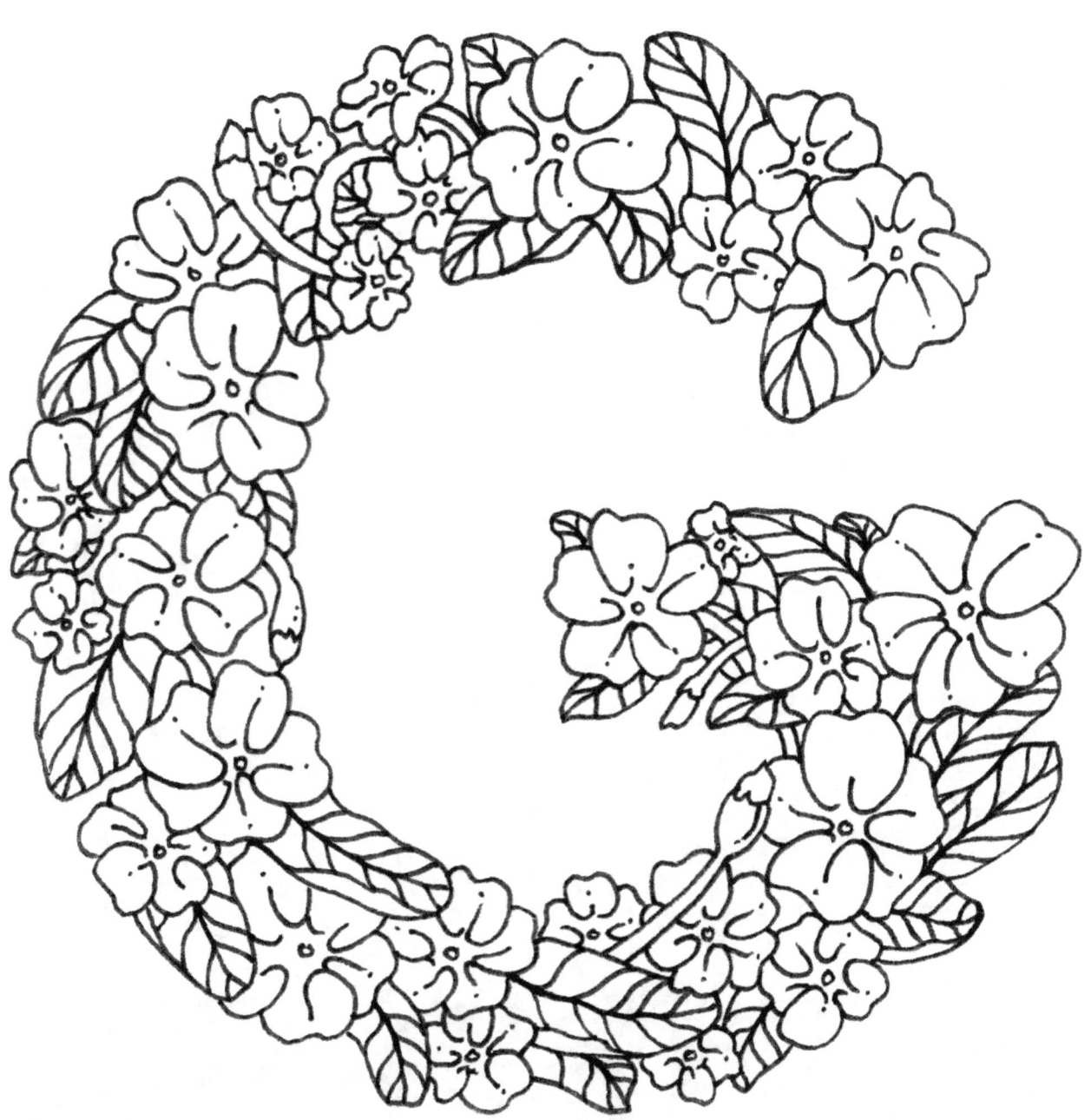

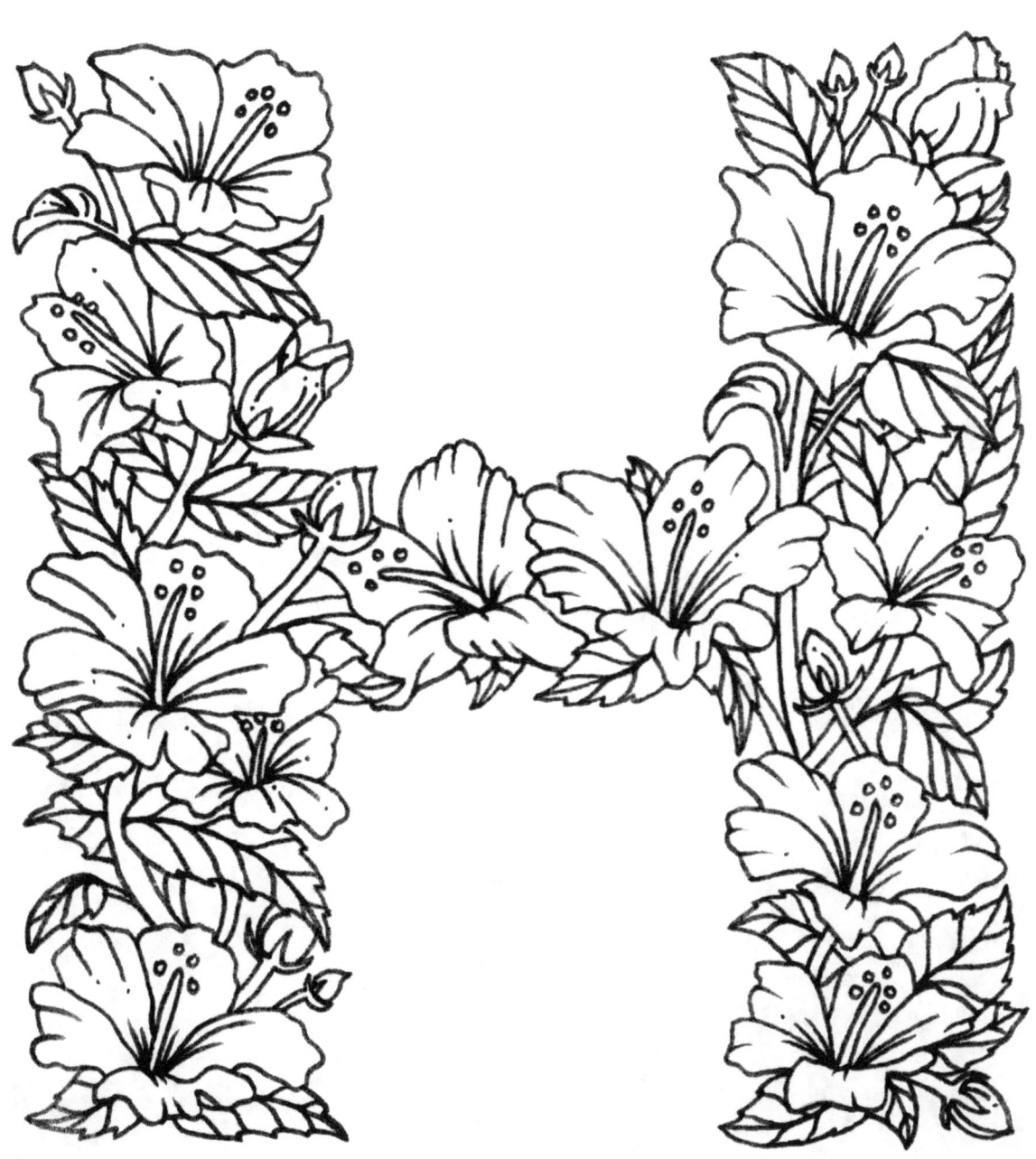

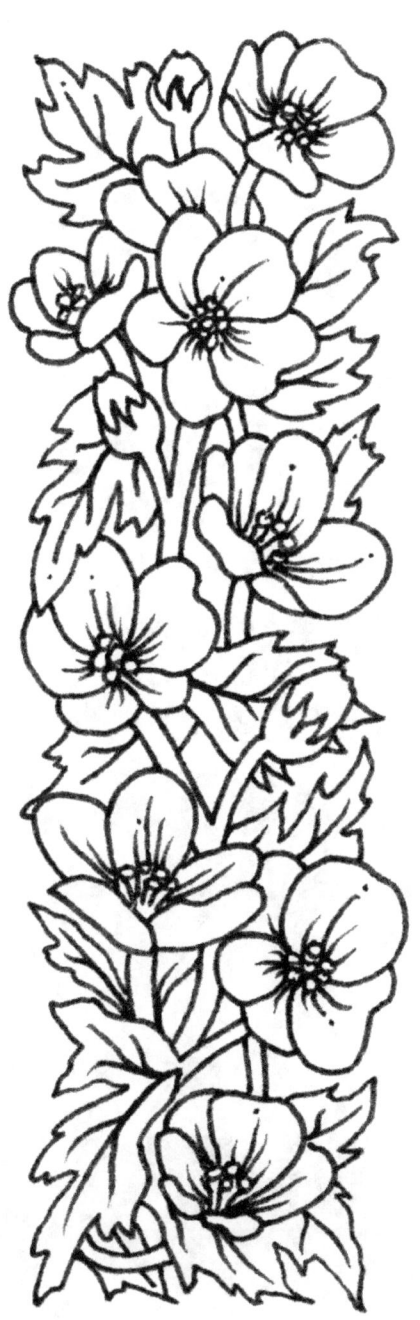

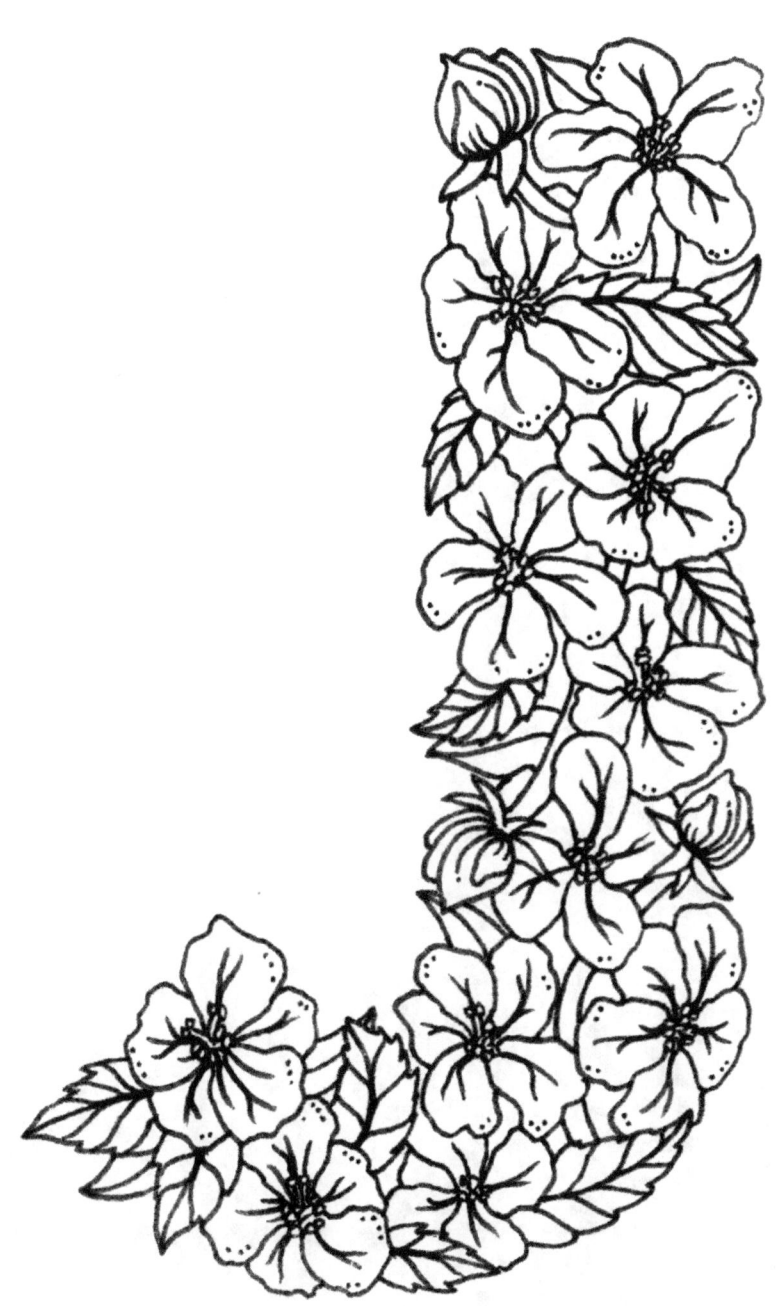

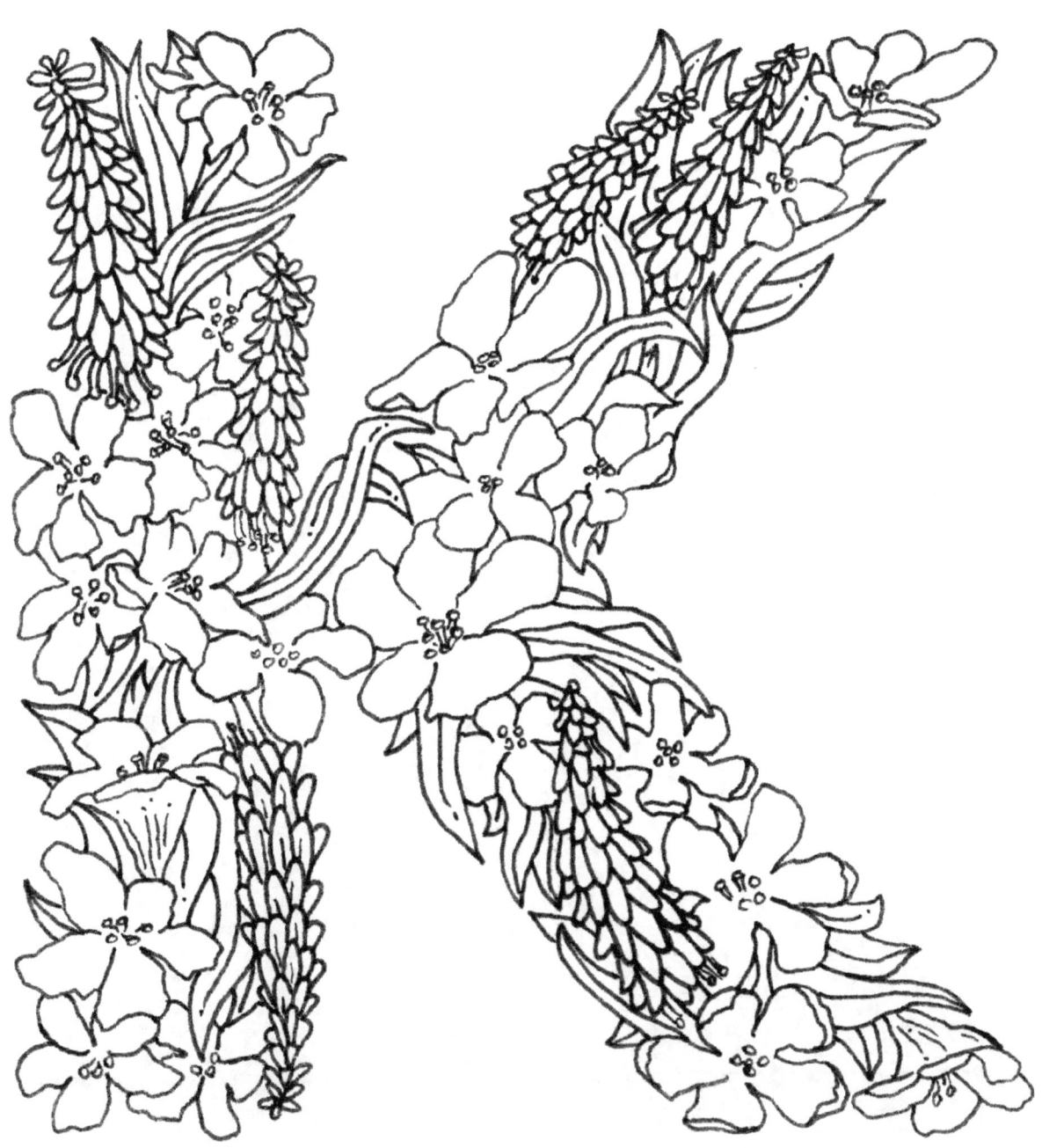

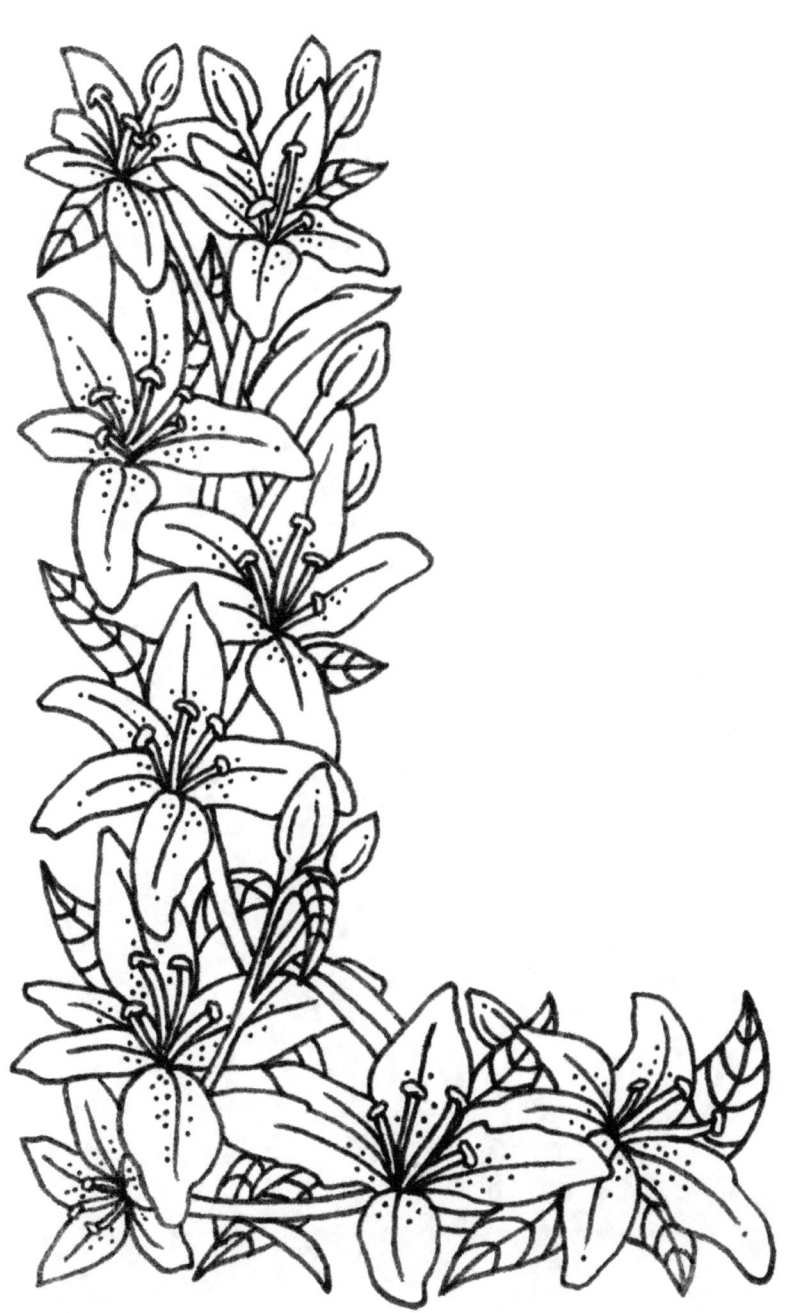

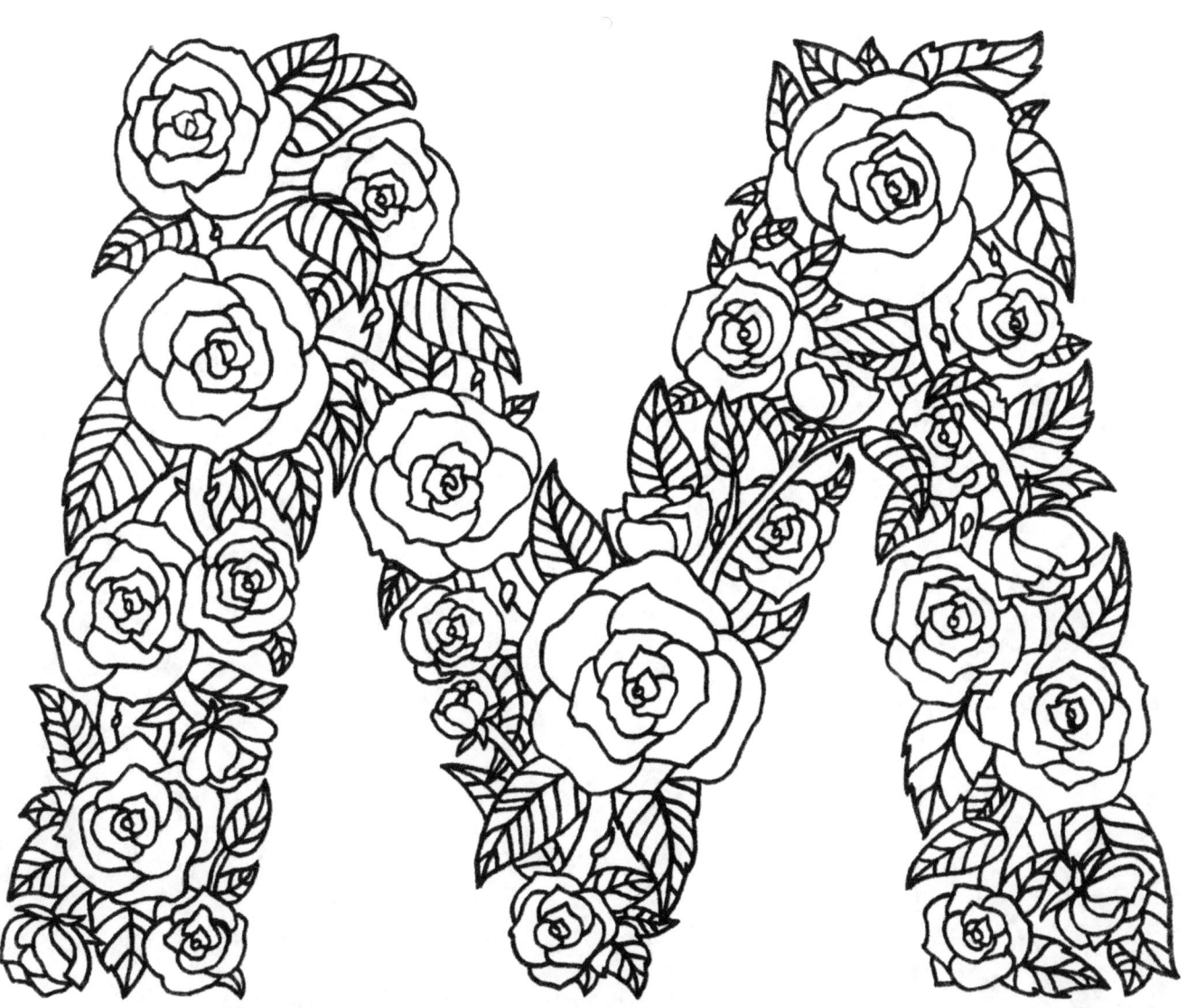

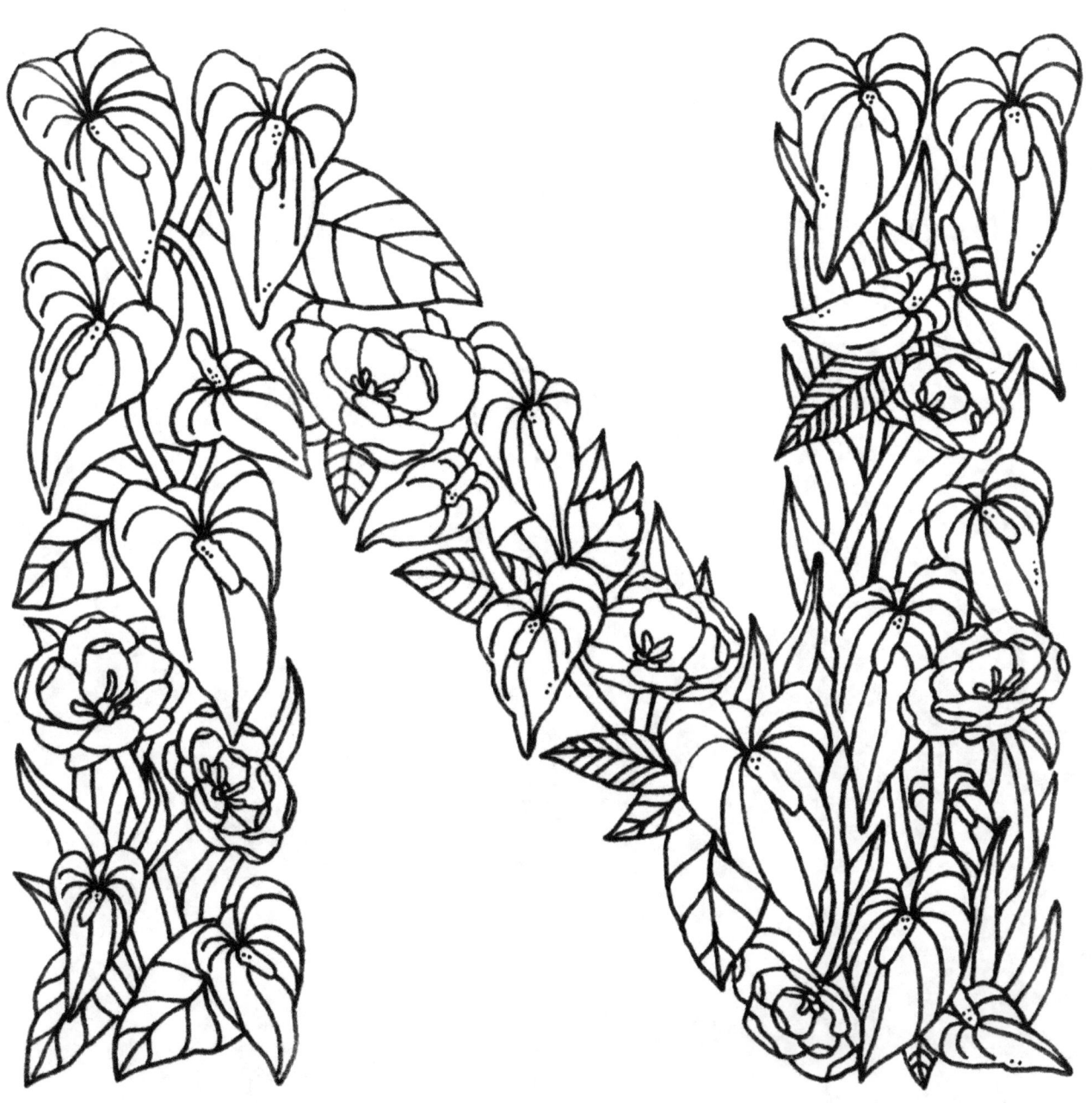

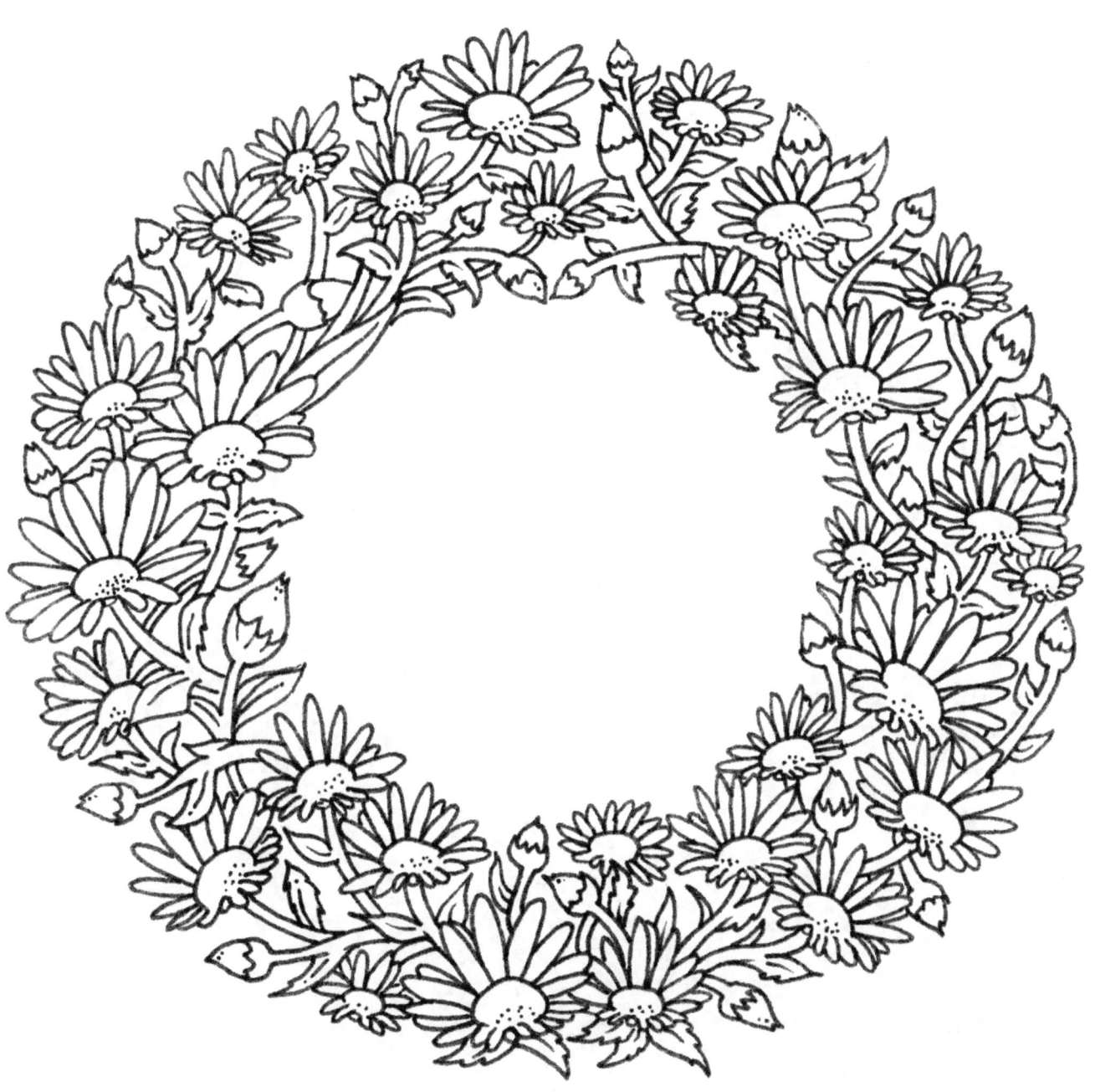

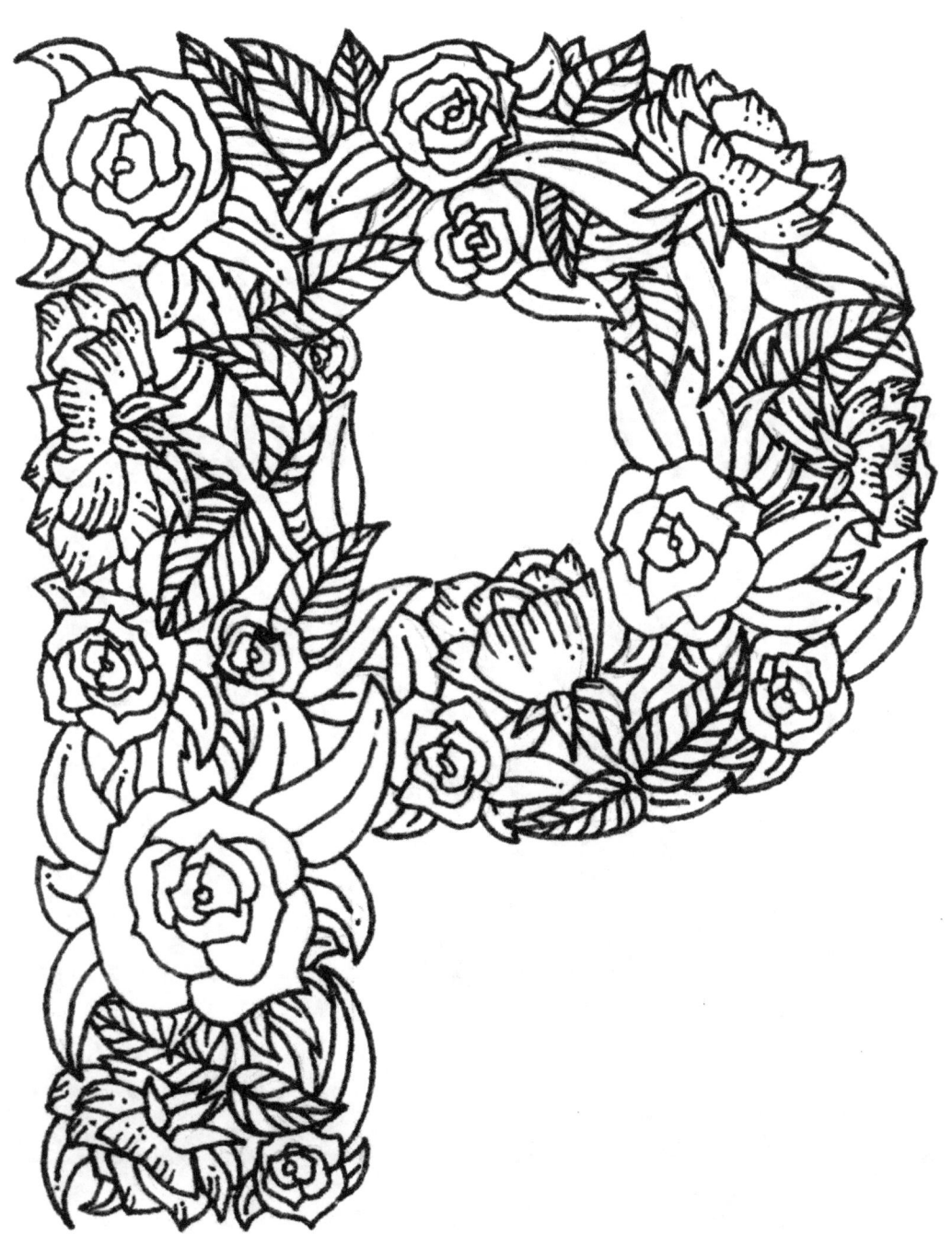

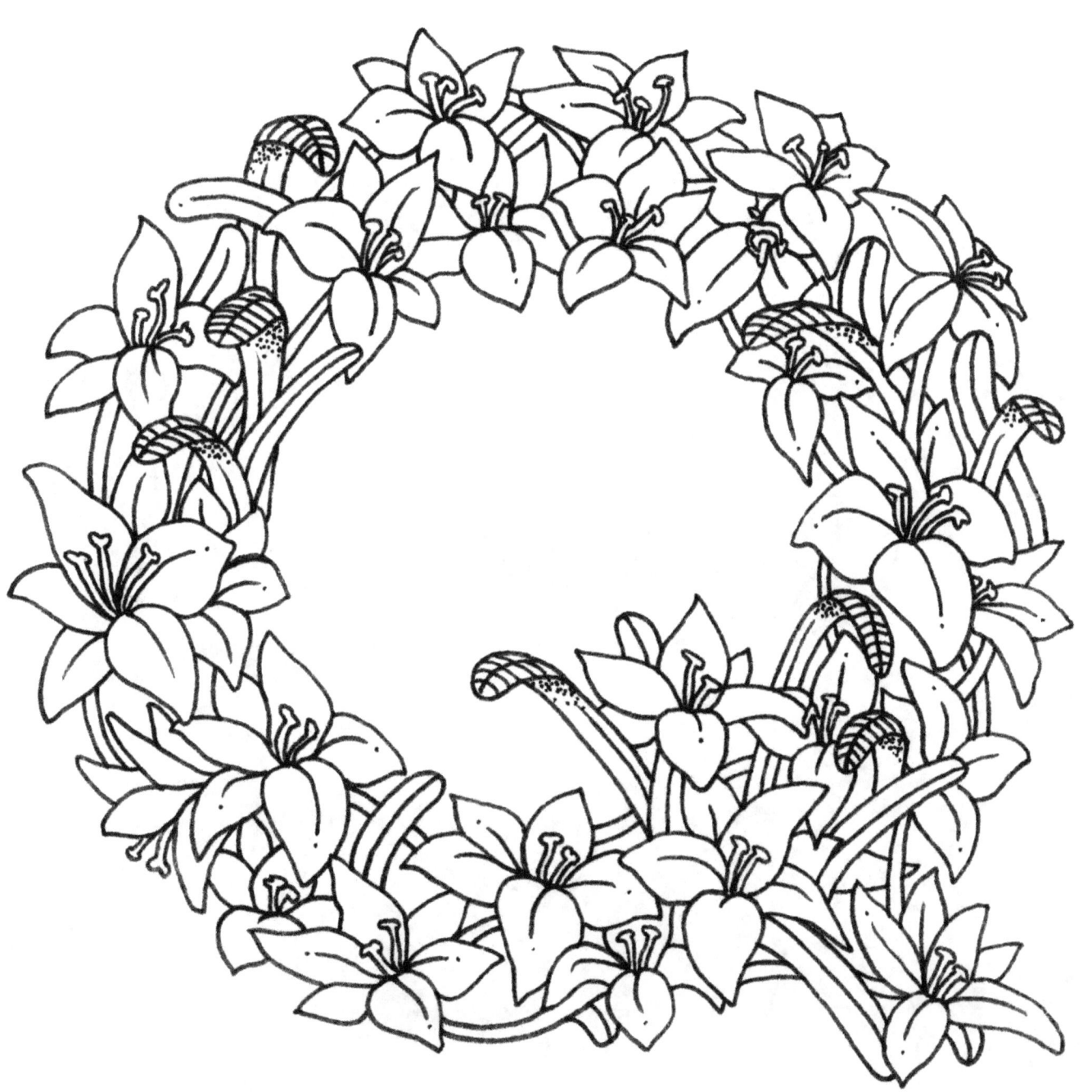

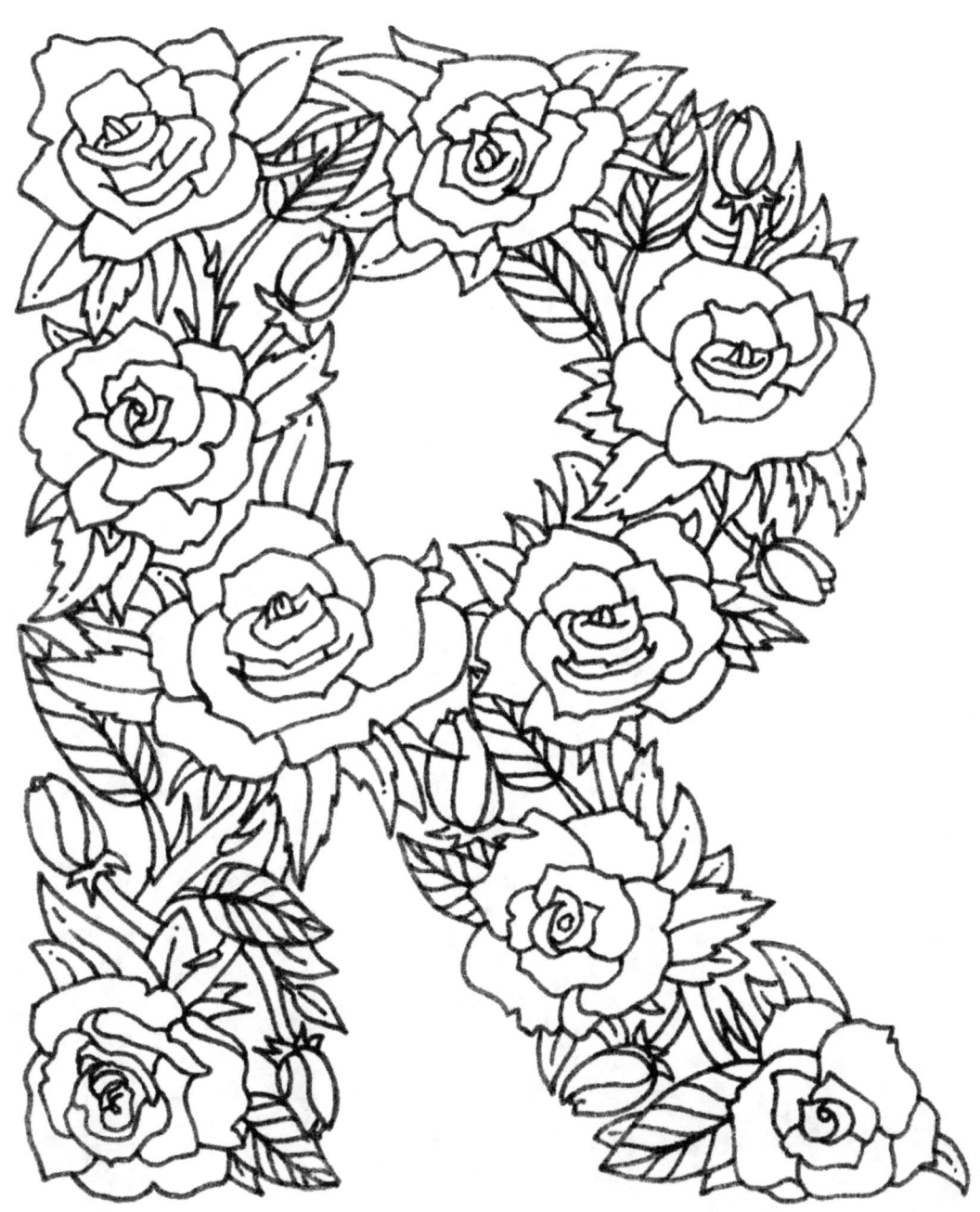

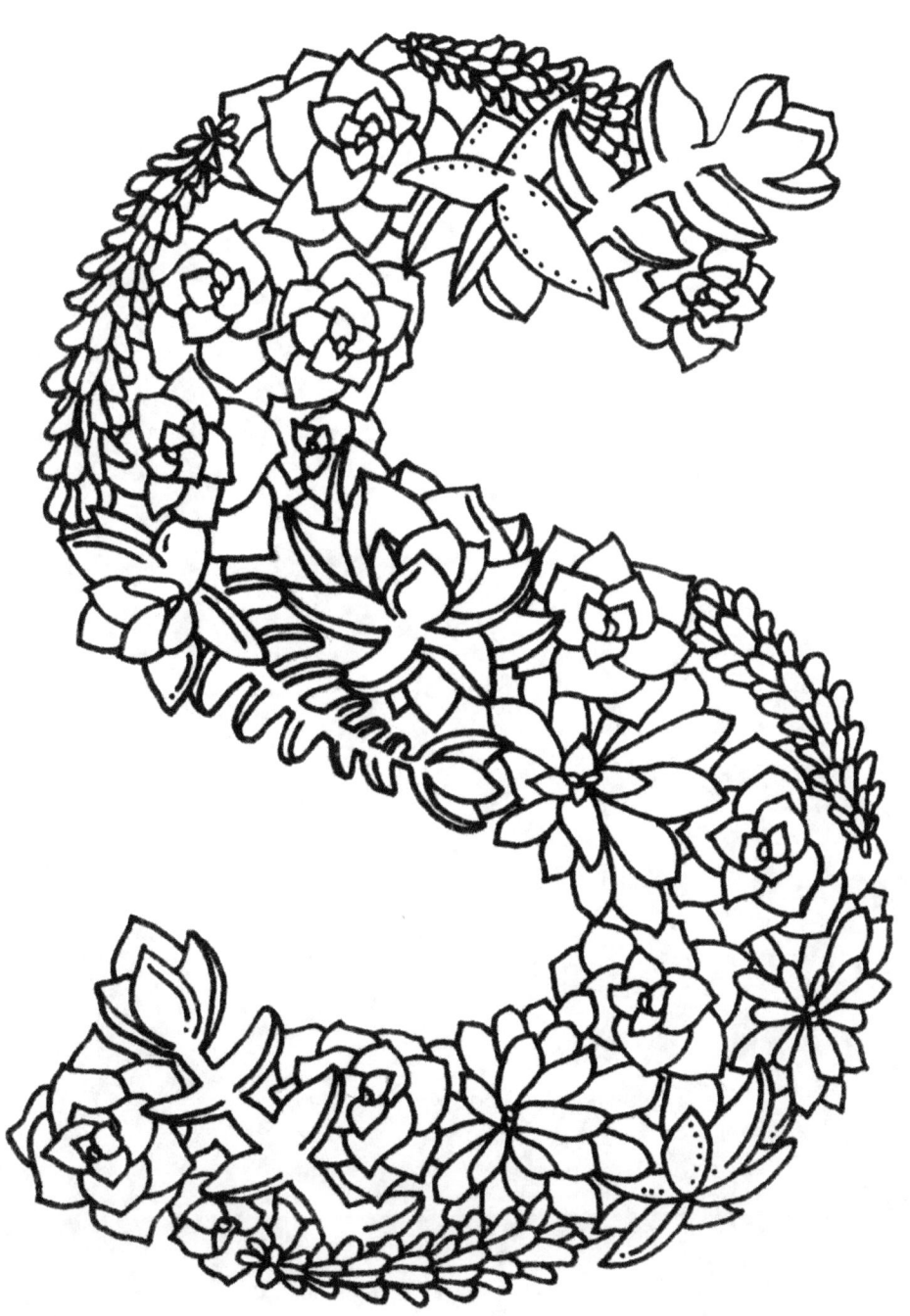

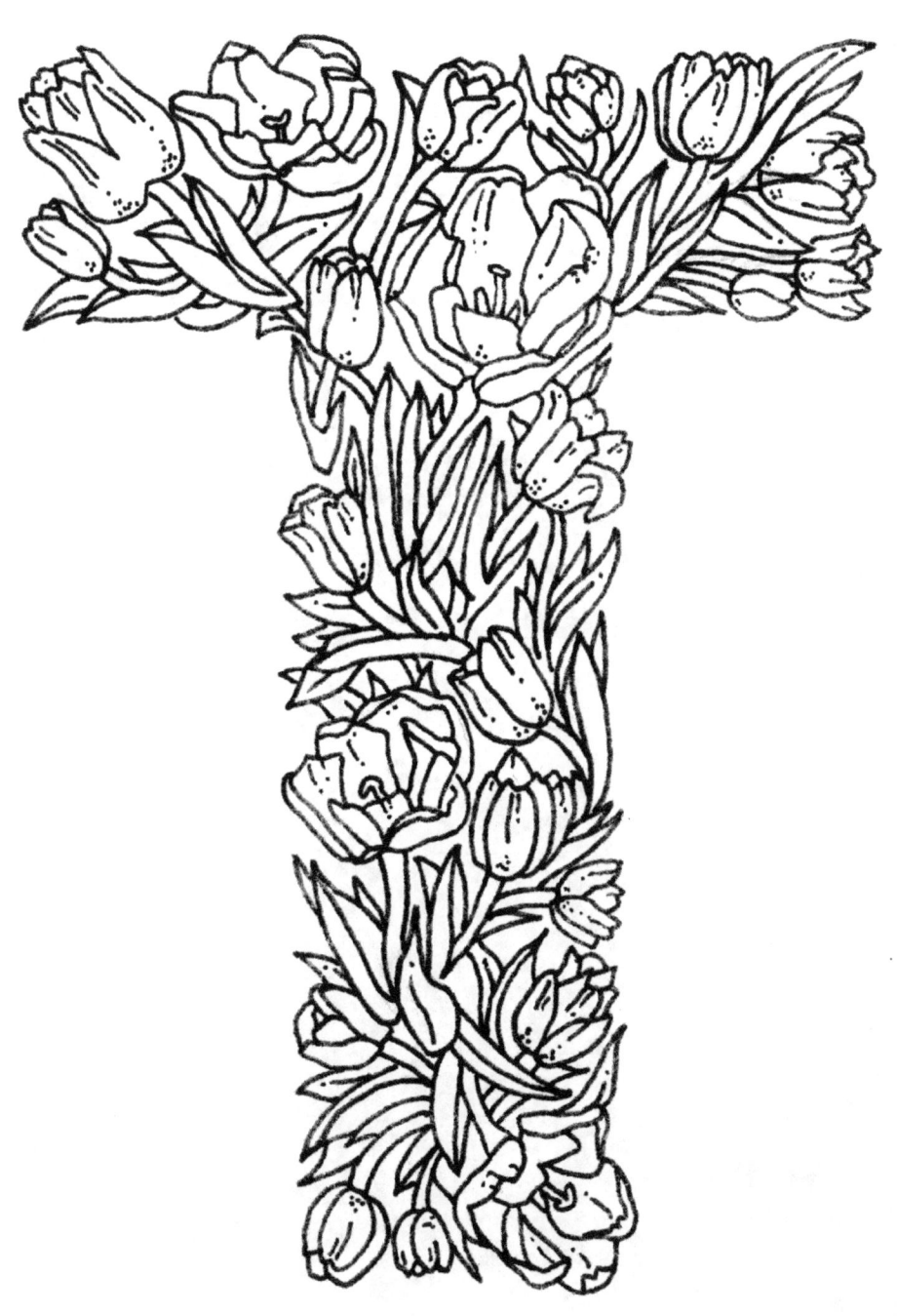

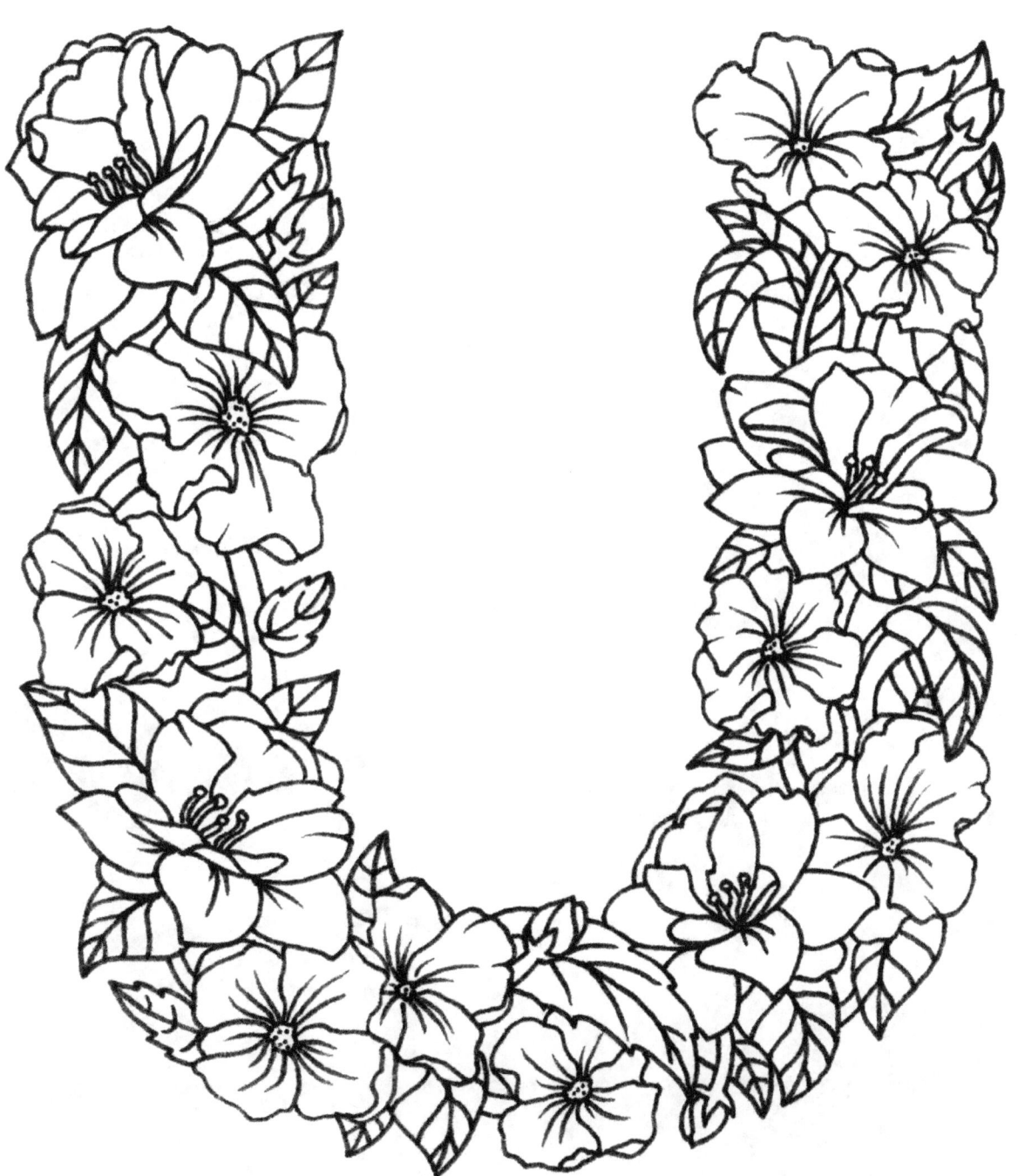

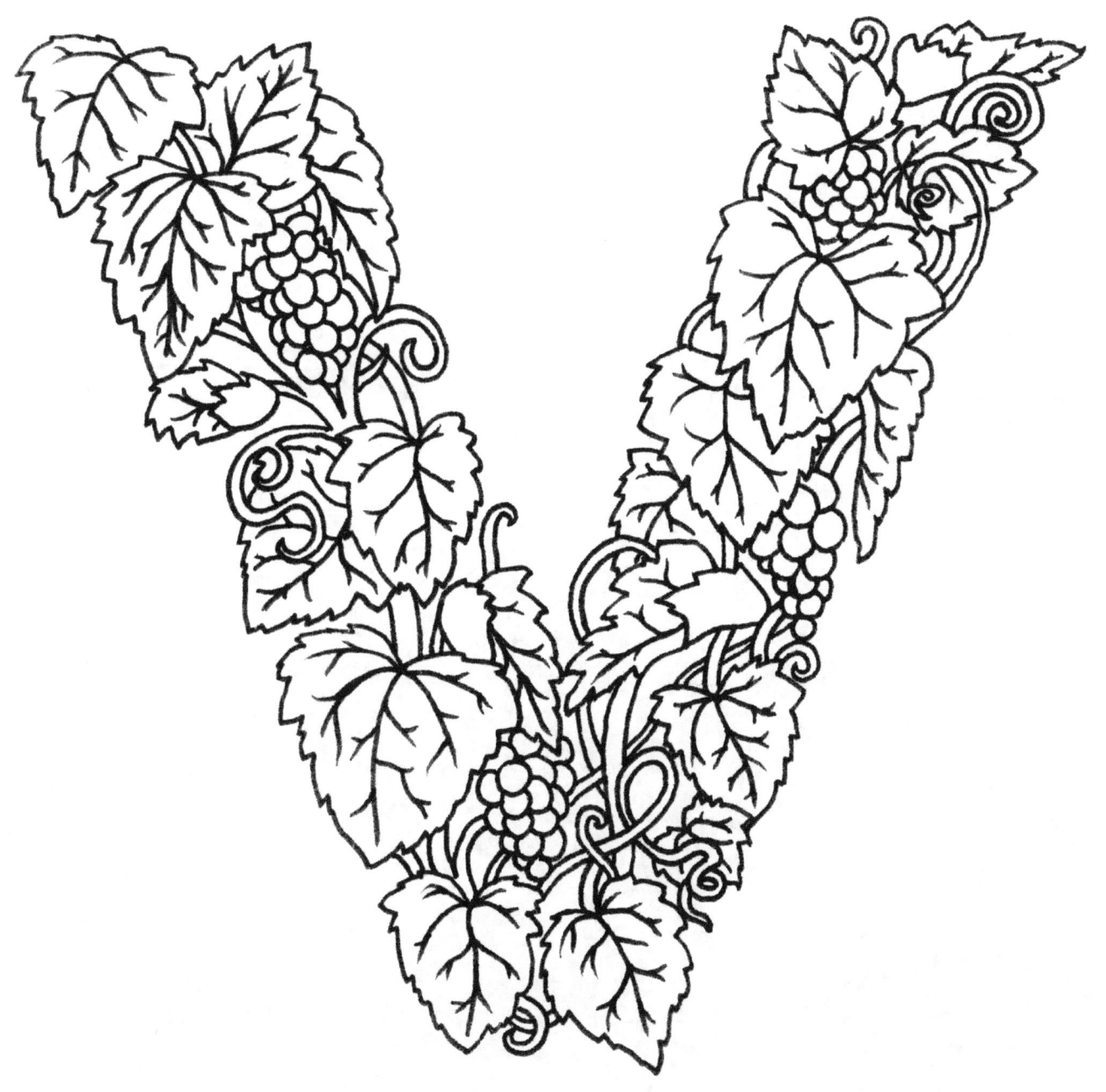

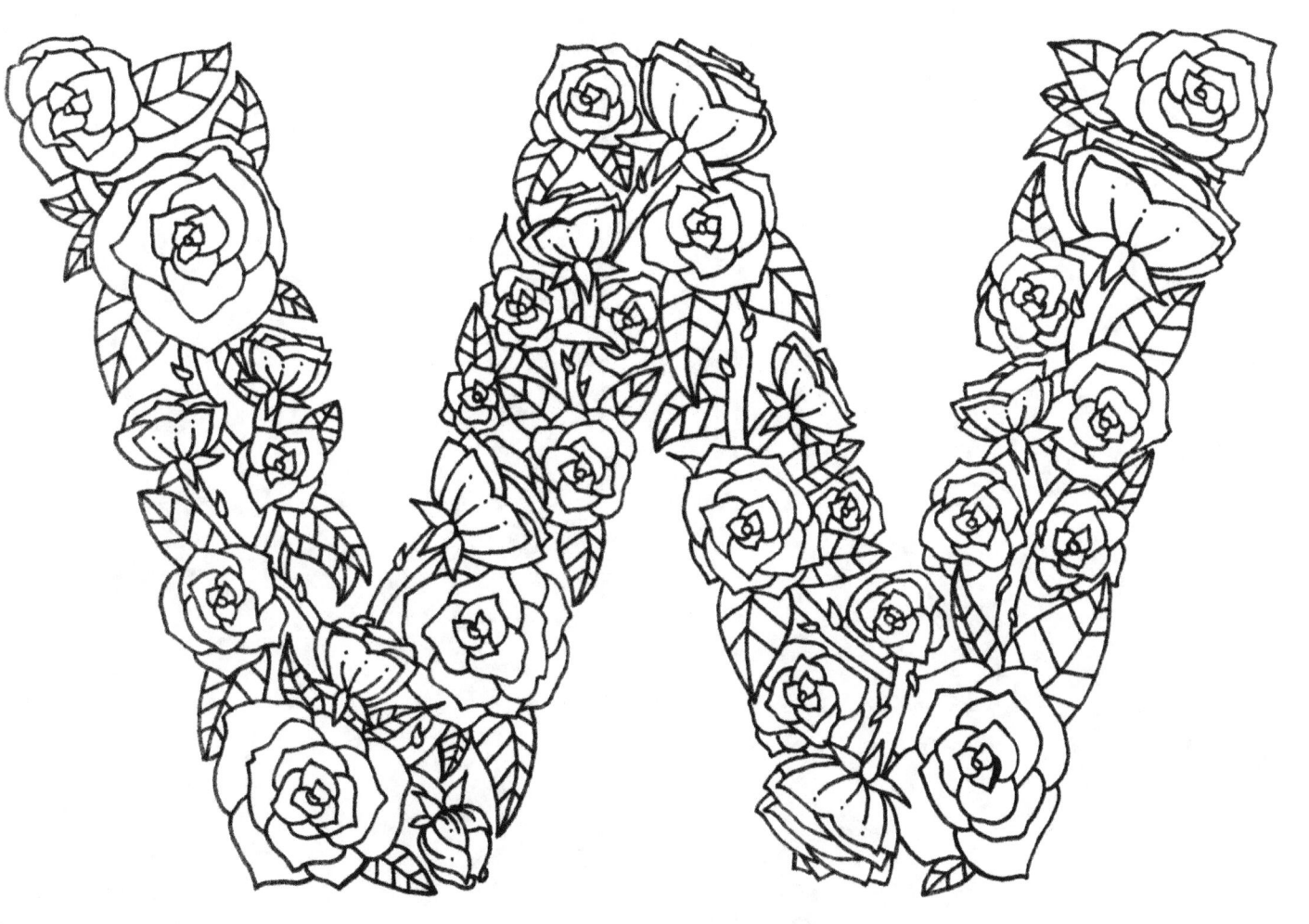

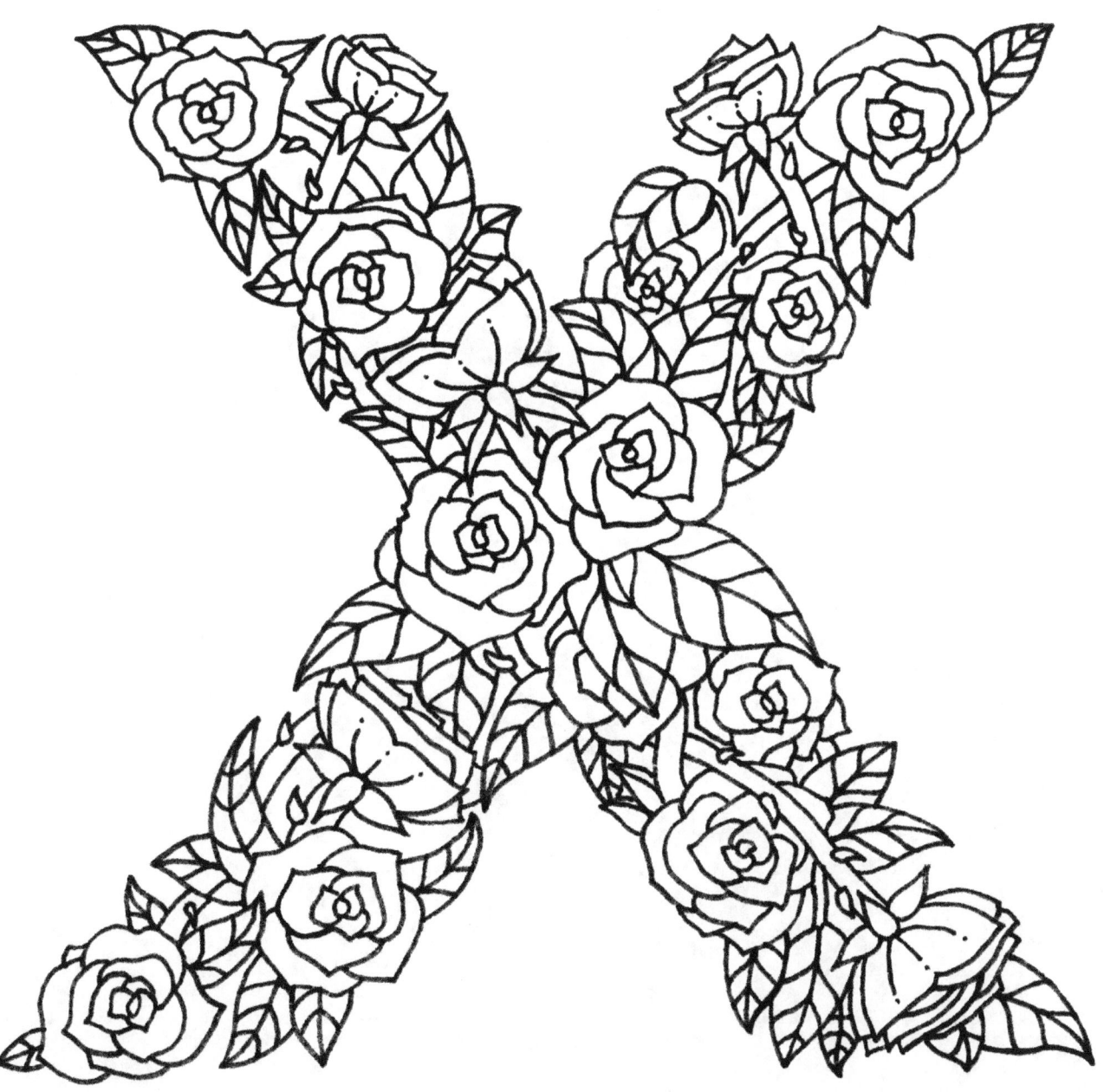

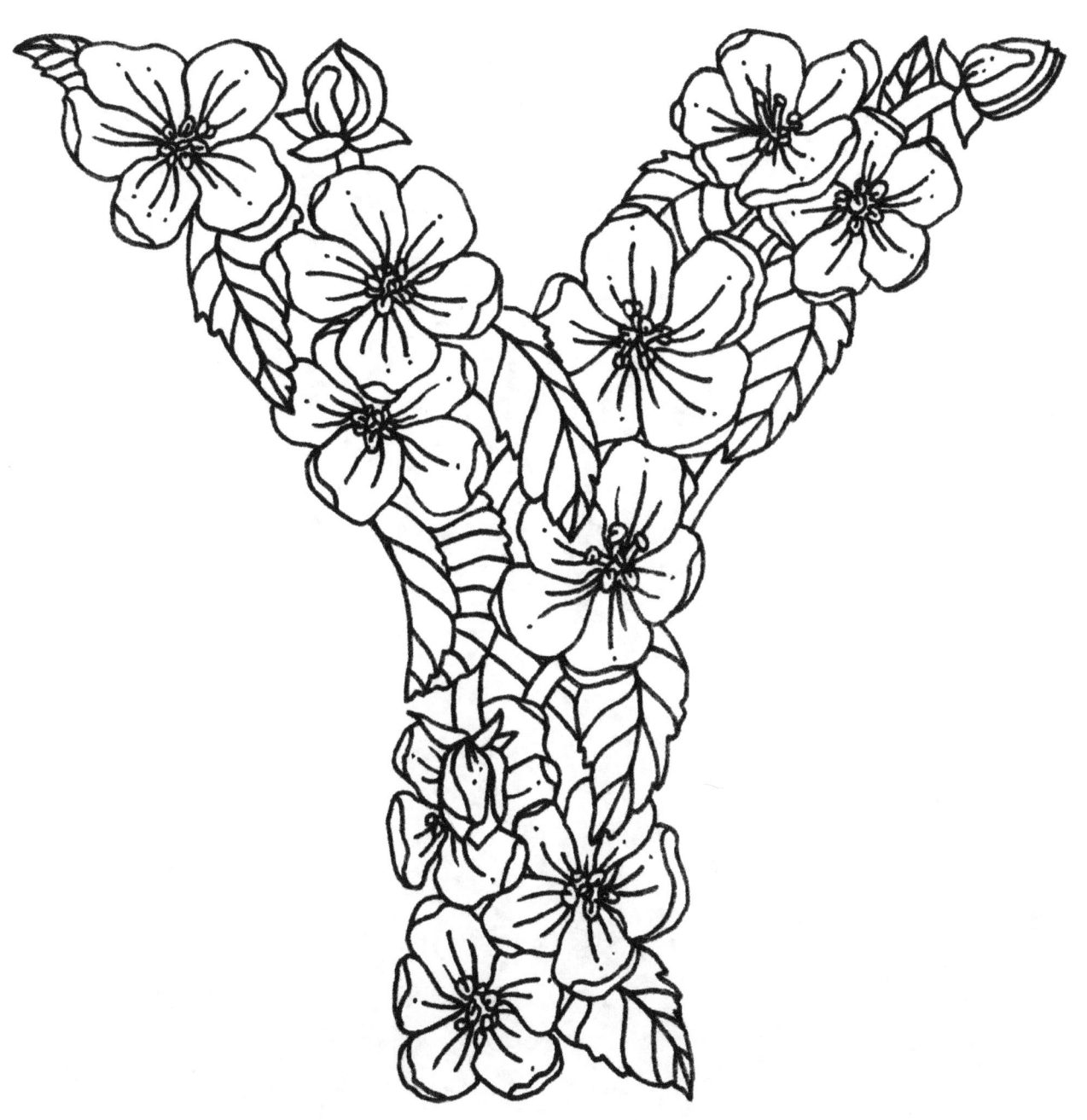

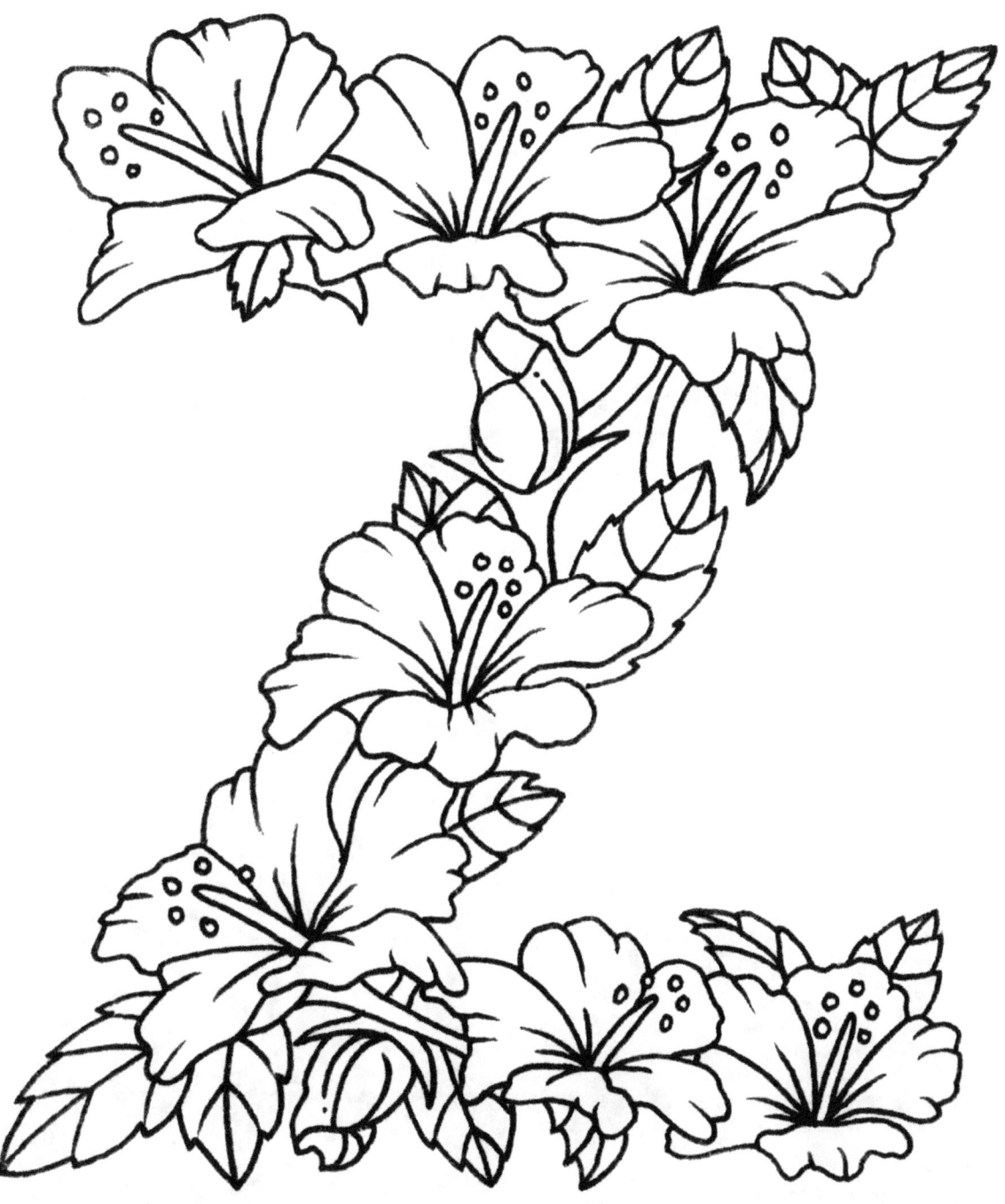

www.ingramcontent.com/pod-product-compliance
Lightning Source LLC
Chambersburg PA
CBHW080842170526
45158CB00009B/2606